THE STRONGHOLD

Sketch of the author by Gene Kloss

THE STRONGHOLD

PHILLIPS KLOSS

Sunstone Press
Santa Fe, New Mexico

FIRST EDITION

Printed in the United States of America

Library of Congress Cataloging in Publication Data:

Kloss, Phillips Wray, 1902-
    The stronghold.

    1. Southwestern States--Poetry. I. Title.
PS3521.L65S76   1986   811'.52   86-14557
ISBN 0-86534-093-5 (hardcover)   ISBN 978-1-63293-149-8 (softcover)

Published in 1987 by Sunstone Press
                    Post Office Box 2321
                    Santa Fe, NM 87504-2321 / USA

CONTENTS

THE STRONGHOLD

PLUMED SERPENT

Aztec Quetzalcoatl, Maya Kukulkàn, Plumed Serpent
A compound concept. bird-snake, sky-earth, Fair God,
Feathered rattlesnake among the Pueblo Indians, Awanyu
Painted on their dance kilts, zigzag lightning thunder-footed
One on the wall of a cliffcave curved like a rainbow
Ghost men dancing under it, Ancestor Spirits
Mixed symbols, mixed meanings, mixed applications.

Marvelous temples were built on the Plumed Serpent motif
Carved stone pediments like hideous gargoyles.
And the priesthood was hideous whatever the god
They ripped out the hearts of living victims with obsidian
        knives
Drowned girls in sky-reflecting water wells
Offerings to the male sungod
Rays penetrating her to perpetuate the people.

The serpent in the Garden of Eden was a more sinister
        symbol
The apples of temptation resulting in slithery impregnation
Hence women fear snakes.

The Cretan snake-goddess an inverse concept
The Greek Medusa's head writhed with evil impulses
The twin-snaked caduceus staff of Mercury headed by paired
        plumed wings
Medical wand of wisdom
Myths, superstitions, credulities, ideologies
Issuing out of the verbal vortex.

9

Factually snakes are very vulnerable.
There are sixty-six species of rattlesnakes, over sixty-six
    subspecies.
Prairie rattlesnakes exposed to the direct rays of sunlight for
    thirty minutes will die.
They seek shade, and desert sidewinders burrow in the sand.
Believe any story you want to believe about .attlesnakes,
    they travel in pairs and if you kill one the mate will
    follow you, git you and bit you.
Some Indian tribes think rattlesnakes are a people like
    red ants.
So what?
Rattlesnakes are rattlesnakes, red ants are red ants.
Brihaspati demolished religious myths and superstitions a
    thousand years before the Toltec-Aztecs concocted the
    Plumed Serpent.
He demolished the gods, the soul, reincarnation, immortality.
You are born, you live, you die, and that's all there is to it,
So eat, drink, indulge your sensual appetites, get as much out
    of life as you can,
Stand on your hind feet like a man, knock down the
    doctrines, dogmas, duties, penances, payments devised
    by priests to keep themselves in power.
Bravo, Brihaspati, 500 B.C., Chaucer alliterated effectively,
    Lucretius hammered hexameters, but without a concept
    of God there can't be a concept of godlessness.
Reality is verbal, positive aspirations as valid as negative
    nihilisms, which Confucius and Lao-tzu well knew.

The Monterey pine
Stands by the sea in storm or shine

Windswept strongbent, hillgirt tall straight
Spreading its branches winnowing fate,
The most beautiful pine in the world, the most,
Native to a narrow strip of California coast,
Transplanted elsewhere in moderate zones
Scattering seeds from its shingled cones.
It is not so magnificent so stately a tree
As the ponderosa pine, its intimacy
Is lovelier than any other pine,
Gracefuller than the flexilis at timberline
Or twisty piñon in the juniper hills.
No pines on the desert where dry heat kills,
Blue-blossomed smoke trees and the indigo burst
Of ironwood tesota quenching eye thirst.
Analogies, metaphors, similes there
In desert, mountain, or ocean air.
The Monterey pine
Stands by the sea in storm or shine,
Mysterious in the mist, Pinus radiata,
Festooned with lichen, Ramalina reticulata.
Words to distinguish, words to construe
Things that seem true
Wildflower meadows, nightflower stars.
Ponder high heaven beyond broken bars
The Plumed Serpent symbol merely a myth
Drawn on a cliff, carved in a glyph.

SUN HAWK

An instantaneous imagination, he improvised his own stories,
elaborated tribal stories, especially bird stories,
Told us about the hummingbird Pai-n-ket-ta-tòl-la who flew
up to the sun and brought golden sunlight down to the
people.
He named himself Sun Hawk, Tol-taw-kae, his grandfather
the great Apache chief Geronimo, his father also named
Geronimo, a powerful Apache medicine man who
married a Taos Indian woman and settled at the pueblo.
A Spanish name, Geronimo, San Geronimo the patron saint
of the pueblo, Indians kept their own names.
Sun Hawk married a Taos girl, Dta-ae, Dancing Leaf, very
beautiful, and he was very handsome. They posed for
artists in town, learned to speak well in English but
thought first in Taos Tiwa, and Sun Hawk understood
Apache Nadine.
He raised corn and wheat, as all Taos Indians did for home
consumption, raised racehorses on the side, won cash
prizes in Ratòn and Colorado race towns.
Whiskey was a problem since the advent of the White Man.
Sun Hawk asked Dta-ae whether he should take the
Whiskey Trail or the Peyote Trail. She said the Peyote
Trail.
It led to complications with the traditional kiva-trained
Indians who didn't like the tent he set up for cult
meetings to the beat of a waterdrum.
Nibbling the peyote button or drinking peyote tea induces
blissful color-visions, charismatic communality, lots of
laughter, giggling, titilations.

His knowledge of medicinal plants, largely inherited from
    his father Old Geronimo, was specific enough, salicylic
    acid in willow bark, aspirin, good for fever as a tea,
And he added something secret to the well known Inmortal
    milkweed, Asclepias asperula, put it in old wine bottles,
    sold it for $25 a bottle, good for lung trouble, stomach
    trouble, heart trouble.
His knowledge of birds was accurate, he knew the Indian
    name of every bird in the Taos Valley, could distinguish
    a Cassin purple finch from a common linnet
    Beel-eez-i-toh.
He assumed the role of sachem, white women were attracted
    to him, age shrank his shoulders, he grew a bit deaf,
    lost his voice, spoke in a whisper,
Walked to town and back every day still the euphoric
    self-named Sun Hawk, his wide-winged imagination
    soaring over the Taos mountains.

SNOW DEER

A strong lean Indian face, furrow lines down from his
nostrils to his mouth-corners, critical penetrating eyes,
wiry fleet-footed physique, Juanito, Snow Deer,
Pahn-paëna.
He belonged to the Chiffunana society, a disciplinary society,
funmakers on fiesta days. They paint black circles
around their eyes, wear cornhusks in their hair, naked
except for loin kilts, torsos painted grey with black
stripes.
Burlesque attire for burlesque tricks. Juanito was the chief
jester. The name Snow Deer didn't seem to fit him.
Perhaps he was born on a deerhide during a snowy
night. Fleet as a deer, yes, a sharp-hoofed sense of
humor.
He was the only Indian who could climb the thick slick
fiesta pole without aid of a ladder halfway up. He
shinnied up it with elastic agility.
Reaching the crosspole near the top he pulled himself onto
it, stood on it silhouette against the sky, danced on it
singing snatches of Indian songs.
His antics on the perilous perch scared the uplooking
spectators breathless, and when he pretended to slip,
men groaned and women screamed.
Recovering he seized the grayed end of a long rope, used
later to lower fiesta gifts tied on the crosspole to the
greedy Chiffunana waiting below, pretended it was a
telephone.
Hallo hallo hallo, you down there with the big Stetson hat,
how many Cadillacs have you-all done got in your lil

19

ole garage in lil ole Tayxas?

Operator, hey operator, connect me with the President of the United States at the White House, will you, please, si gusta? I wanna tell him off!

Swinging himself down by the rope he strutted toward the Catholic shrine at the west end of the Indian dance-ground and footrace track. It was a bower of green and gold aspen branches set on a raised platform. He strutted in front of it sanctimoniously.

The crowd had gathered in a guarded line along the dance-ground watching the other Chiffunana play outrageous pranks. Juanito took the stage, leaped on the platform, faced the crowd, chanted in a big deep voice like a Catholic priest a litany of English swearwords.

Abruptly he jumped down, mingled with the Chiffunana, and they danced a mock Indian dance with exaggerated steps, burlesquing their own ceremonies and own religion.

He was a first-rate farmer, expert fence-builder, often worked for the ranchers around Eagle Nest Lake, one of them letting him run his small herd of unbranded stock with the branded herefords.

He disdained posing for artists but permitted his daughter Evalina to pose for Gene, a mysterious-eyed girl, secretive eyelashes, secretive smile.

Gene found her an intelligent model, quite confidential, though she never betrayed any Indian esoteric. Gene etched a very subtle likeness of her on copper plate.

Our friendship with Juanito was based on tacit trust and Evalina's intermediacy. We never inquired his official status at the Pueblo, never inquired the status of the Chiffunana.

21

They are not analogous to the Koshairi of the Keresan
   pueblo of Santo Domingo, the so-called Delight Makers,
   Ancestor Spirits. They have authority but their function
   is obscure.
"My father is a good man," said Evalina, and we agreed,
   sufficient status for us.
He took care of an orphan Indian boy, trained him the star
   performer of his dance troupe, educated him, took care
   of his own family, his own people.
Snow Deer! He left no footprints in the snow but he did
   leave the imprint of a nonpareil character.

RED DEER

He was chopping wood for the auto court, a clean-looking
   Indian, blanket wrapped around his waist, two neat
   braids of hair hanging down his shirtfront.
There was no electricity in Taos in those days, the board-
   and-batten cabins of the auto court were equipped with
   a kerosene lamp, wash basin, water pitcher, dump
   bucket, and wood-burning stove.
Crude but clean and airy, screen porches, discreet outhouses,
   the best accommodations in town, iron bedsteads, hard
   mattresses.
The Indian stopped chopping to sit on a log and refresh
   himself with an Indian song, using a piece of wood he
   had chopped as a drumstick to beat on the ground.
He had a wonderful voice, resonant baritone, vigorous,
   virile. We listened spellbound, rewarded him with a cup
   of coffee and jelly sandwich, talked with him.
It was the beginning of a lifelong friendship. He invited us
   to come to his house at the Pueblo, told us it was the
   one between the church and the stream, we couldn't
   miss it.
A cozy house, pitchpine fire in the fireplace, kitchen
   divided off by a bench-like adobe wall, his wife and
   daughter as friendly as he. We learned their names
   casually.
His was Adam, his wife's was Marie, his daughter's Rosita,
   their Indian names Red Deer, Pai-paëna, Elk Woman,
   Tu-u-una, and Chokecherry, Ook-tu-ka-lae.
He kept a team of horses and wagon in his corral, raised
   wheat, threshed it on the community threshing machine,

had it ground into flour at the thumping steam-engine
mill in Taos.

Marie baked round loaves of Indian bread in her outdoor
adobe oven, delicious bread, and Adam obtained meat
hunting deer and rabbits or trading at the stores in town.
He sold moccasins, drums, flutes to the tourists at the
Pueblo.

Like Snow Deer he trained a trio dance-troupe, performed at
the Don Fernando hotel and private parties, Circle
Dance, War Dance, Shield Dance, Hoop Dance.

They won prizes at the Gallup intertribal pow-wow, were
solicited by commerical organizations at Phoenix, college
groups at Tempe and Tucson, the Fire Dance his
specialty.

He posed for Gene in dance regalia, helped build our house
on the mesa by the old Mahualukimo Indian trail over
to the buffalo plains, taught us a song belonging to that
house.

He was always affable, always greeted us in store or street
with the phrase Ee-ah-ho, puiu, broadly interpreted How
goes the world with you, my friend.

His life was a continuous song to the beat of an invisible
drum, and when two sons were born his zest was
unquenchable, he taught them the whole repertoire of
Indian songs and dances.

Pat's Indian name was Nu-ku, Good Night, because the night
he was born was a good night, Jim's name was Nu-po,
Night Rain, because it rained the night he was born, a
good omen.

They were both top dancers, Pat the champion Hoop Dancer
of America till a bullet in the Korean war grazed his

spine and paralyzed his left leg.

An adjustable family. Pat learned to make handcarved furniture, Jim joined the Air Force, master sergeant, Rosita married a Navaho.

Adam learned to drive a car, took his dance troupe and handicrafts to outlying markets, made money. His cedar and redwood flutes were playable in scale, sweet-toned, and were bought by collectors at high prices. He became famous, stayed modest.

He was elected Governor of the Pueblo in his seventies, helped reconcile the older and younger factions, always constructive, always affable wherever he was.

Should he and Marie, Gene and me meet again in an Elysian aftermath, I am sure we would hear him greet us from behind a pile of star-wood Ee-ah-ho, puiu.

Adam, our old friend Adam Red Deer!

THE WOMAN WHO MARRIED AN INDIAN

She was a conspicuity seeker, celebrity hunter, she drew
    artists and writers around her to draw attention to
    herself, built guest houses for them, dispensed largesse
    like a queen.

Born an only child of posh parents she grew up thinking
    she could buy anything she wanted. She collected four
    husbands, the last a Taos Indian not so riddable as the
    first three.

'Twas said she payed his Indian wife a stipend to release him,
    or rather to lease him, and she adopted his Spanish
    name Lujan, changing the j to h to read Luhan.

She wrote checks under the name Mable Luhan, wrote books
    under the name Mabel Luhan, distributed favors under
    the name Mabel Luhan, and was jocosely dubbed
    Queen Mabel.

She built an adobe palace wth a glass gazebo on top for her
    Indian consort, toted him with her to New York, his
    Indian blanket and braided hair adding to her
    conspicuity.

A strong likeable character nevertheless, Tony Luhan,
    capable, courteous, a British accent he had picked up
    from the English gentleman Arthur Manby and the
    Honorable Dorothy Brett, one of Mabel's coterie in the
    D.H. Lawrence days.

She had inveigled Lawrence to come to Taos, gave him a
    ranch at the foot of the Lobo mountains in exchange
    for one of his manuscripts, tried to detach him from
    his German wife Frieda.

Frieda saw through her, hung on to him till he died of T.B.

in France, then brought his ashes back for burial at the ranch. Apparently he loved the ranch, proclaimed the view across the Rio Gande to the uplift of the Continental Divide the most beautiful landscape in the world.

It was his will to have his ashes buried there. Frieda brought them back in an unsealed urn. Mabel stole some of the ashes for a necrophiliac keepsake.

Frieda retrieved them, threatening a lawsuit, mixed them with concrete, buried the slab on the ranch, built a shrine over it, and hundreds of women who had wallowed vicariously in Lawrence's novels made pilgrimmages to the shrine to worship a sex-god.

Sterile sex-god. All his novels were repetitive extensions of his autobiographical *Sons and Lovers*, all his women were the same woman perpetually frustrated, all his men the same himself perpetually frustrated.

He never knew the meaning of the word love, except love of the land. Mabel wasn't frustrated, but her real love was love of the Taos country, Tony an indigenous part of it.

Lawrence's demise impelled her to look for another sex-writer to vanitize her domain. The Carmel poet Robinson Jeffers was available, his incestuous story *Tamar* qualified him a lurid trophy to hang on her literary wall.

She invited him and his wife Una to be her guests in the big house, the palace. They liked Taos, liked Tony, who chauffeured them around the country in Mabel's Chrysler Imperial.

Jeffers identified himself with the rock head of Taos

Mountain looking down on the activites of Indians and
   White man. He wrote that only he and the Mountain
   understood civilization was an ephemeral disease.
Mable was tempted to put a dent in such a lofty granite
   attitude, invited them again the next summer along
   with a former flame of his.
The flame reignited. Una, older than Jeffers, felt she was
   being cast aside, so during one of Mabel's evening
   parties she went to her room and shot herself with
   a pistol.
Tony heard the shot, told Jeffers. Jeffers rushed to their
   room, saw Una bleeding on the bed but not dead,
   swept her up in his arms and figuratively carried
   her back to Carmel.
They lived happily ever after till Una died of cancer and
   Jeffers took up with Judith Anderson, the actress who
   made a great success of his melodramatic version of
   Euripedes' *Medea*.
Mabel arranged worser melordramers, instigated
   divorces among the Taos artists, Victor Higgins,
   John Young-Hunter, Nicolai Fechin, her own
   divorces a precedent, quite a mischief-maker.
On her better side she was very generous, helped artists,
   Indians, poverty-stricken families financially, helped the
   Indians with their land claims, John Collier appointed
   commissioner, and she was beset by moochers.
She built a house for Willa Cather, who rejected it, so
   Mabel donated it to a society of Polish Sisters for a
   hospital, and she tried to bring appreciative people to
   her beloved Taos.
Though she clashed with Georgia O'Keeffe she was a
   perfect hostess to responsive celebrities such as Max

Eastman, A.A. Brill, Greta Garbo and Leopold Stokowski, the Vanderbilts, dozens of movers and shakers.

She might have been the right wife for Lawrence at that. He was the only one who loved the country as she did, every sagebrush, every rabbitbush, the incomparable views.

When Tony died and she suffered a slight dementia she hired a chauffeur to drive her around and around the Taos Valley communing with her favorite places.

She is buried in the historic Kit Carson Cemetery, an inconspicuous headstone marking her grave, often knocked down by local maurauders, reset by her friends.

Lawrence's ashes remain enshrined at the ranch she gave him, a cenotaph monument erected for him at Westminster Abbey.

THE GREATEST ARTIST IN TAOS

"Is Mr. Fleck really the greatest artist in Taos?" inquired
    the naive little lady from Texas.
"Well, he's good but I wouldn't say he was the greatest. Did
    somebody tell you he was?"
"Yes, *he* did!" said the naive little lady from Texas, the
    greatest state in the union till Alaska greatered it.
Bert, Blumy, and Berny, the three B's like Bach, Beethoven,
    and Brahms were considered the greatest artists in Taos,
    Bert Greer Phillips. Ernest L. Blumenschein, Oscar E.
    Berninghaus.
Later Victor Higgins was considered tops, then Andrew
    Dasburg with his Lord Byron limp and crisp supercilious
    accent was acclaimed the great master.
His progress from Cézanne through synchromism to stark
    triangles set on a sliding diagonal plane simulating Taos
    peaks set on a slanting plain entitled him to preeminence.
Bert Phillips certainly knew the most about the Taos Indians,
    idyllized them a bit, singer in the moonlight, flute
    player in the moonlight, man wooing maid in a
    meadow,
His portraits more extractive and exactive, his group pictures
    humanitarian, and he excelled in his color modulations.
Blumenschein had a chunky style, basaltic blocks in the Rio
    Grande Gorge, sage clumps, cloud clumps, contrapuntal
    Indian dance lines, strong colors, solid structure,
    dynamic designs.
Berninghaus depicted local scenes, cowboy horses tethered
    outside a lamp-lit saloon on a cold winter night, fiesta
    crowd on a hot summer day, the shimmer of heat
    visible in the painting.

Joseph Sharp resorted to photographs for his pictures of tipi
    tribes but his studies of Taos Indians were direct, his
    Taos landscapes spontaneous, impressionistic, livable.
By the same token John Young-Hunter, who painted elegant
    society portraits, a powerful one of Winston Chruchill,
    freed himself in his superlative watercolor sketches.
Walter Ufer's colors have stayed brighter than the colors of
    any other Taos artist, pure pigment out of the tube, lots
    of punch, faulty posturing.
Compared to the Old Masters of the Renaissance the Taos
    artists at least had original subject-matter uncorrupted
    by vapid Madonnas, Pietas, nudes, allegorical figures,
And they still hold their own against modernistical braggarts
    and swaggarts, against fads, cults, coteries, workshops,
    their art individualistic.
The second congeries of Taos artists, beginning in the 1920's,
    thrived on the fame of the first group, stricter in their
    objectives, some trying to get the essence of a thing,
    others striving for flagrant conspicuity, and money.
The money value of art, the prestige of price and pretense
    of profundity that goes with it, has nothing to do with
    the greatness of art.
Titian's portraits, even in reproductions, quite apart from his
    reclining nude, reveal an insight no other artist ever
    expressed, a timeless significance, each one a
    masterpiece, the value instrinsic.

THREE MANIFESTOS QUOTED VERBATIM

"With regard to painting of today I am favorably inclined to
what is going on. I find my best work has been
motivated by spontaneous preoccupation with
antagonistic forms associated and harmonized through
subject-matter. That the result is figurative troubles
me not at all."

"My work from the beginning has had two underlying
elements, one the basic architectonic structure of design
relating to the orchestration of form and color, the
other the truth as I have experienced the life of
contemporary man and portrays him in his
environment."

"The singular vision in painting is no longer relevant today.
Man is dealing with multiplicity, a conglomeration of
ideas, visually diffused and yet plastically coherent. Man
and art are too technically advanced to be content with
mere genre statements. Only individuals can and will
survive from the vast technocratic society that is
engulfing us. Art is the stabilizer wherein man can be
assured of reality. There is a vast difference between
the reality of the eye and the reality of the psyche. I am
not content with man or nature, they are temporary. I
prefer working with the dark abysses of the mind."

APPASSIONATA

Music is thought transcending verbal significance
A phrase in different settings accretes contextual meaning
Major implies minor, mood implies mood
The sudden syncopation in the Appassionata
Splits tempo, tone, structure apart
The phrase tying it together ending on a single note
Feeling and thought surge through the heart and head
Immortal music, Beethoven dead.

DUET WITH A COYOTE

The old gravel pit was deep and wide
Rimmed with sagebrush on every side
Mountains rimming the sky beyond.
We made it a glade, a place to respond
To quietness hidden from traffic and town.
Rabbits and quail came wandering down
And once a coyote trotting along the rim
Yapped just to yap, so I yapped at him.
He stopped and saw me sitting on a rock
And yapped to test whether I would mock.
I did, and we joined in a plaintive duet
Howling for things we could never get.
No doubt he scented I was gunless and harmless
And trotted away, no need for alarmness.
Often beset by complexities I
Feel in rapport with the coyote's cry.

LONE CHIPMUNK

Nose to nose with a vesper sparrow
He nibbles the grain we put there to share so
With birds and rabbits, wary of cats.
He stuffs his pouches for his storage vats,
Usually alone except when chasing
Other chipmunks playfully racing.
He scoots and scampers, chatters and churrs,
Summer the season for hims and hers.
When snowbirds arrive he is always alone,
Sits up straight, long tail prone,
Contemplates leaves falling gold on the ground
Winter soon coming, bleak, icebound,
No mate to nest with or chip at or cheep
Long hibernation, nothing but sleep.
His loneliness seems so pathetic appealing
We wish we could house him under our ceiling.

WILLOW WANDS

Bare stems of willow bright in the snow
Red blue and yellow wave to and fro
Wands making magic of all that you know
Flicked bare and bright in the white winter glow.

CREST OF THE CONTINENT

Monarch Pass, the Royal Gorge of the Arkansas river east,
   Black Canyon of the Gunnison river west, the crest of
   the continent continuing north and south.
Not an isostasy of height and depth, the Himalaya mountains
   the highest in the world, the Mariana Trench the lowest
   ocean depth, not an isostasy.
Various viewpoints of grandeur from a crest, various
   elevations, forms, substances, dwarf blue forget-me-nots,
   the exquisite fragrance of tiny white primrose.

ECHO CAVE

The massive sandstone cliffs of the Wingate Formation in the
    Chama river basin are arched with shallow caves.
Atop the Wingate is the gypsum Todilto Formation, atop the
    Todilto the radioactive Morrison Formation loaded with
    agatized and opalized fossils.
Below the Wingate is the loose shale Chinle Formation,
    amethyst in it, on down to primordial granites and
    schists.
The caves seem to echo the geologic ages, and they actually
    do echo the sounds along the Old Spanish Trail to Los
    Angeles, now a paved highway.
The large cave across from Ghost Ranch is a veritable
    megaphone. Yell to hell with Santa Claus at Christmas
    and it will repeat your blasphemy loudly and clearly.
Or choose a politican you don't like and lay it on thick,
    the cave will echo your opinions with gratifying
    distinctness.

JOHN DUNN'S BRIDGE

Gambler, gunfighter, bridge builder, stage driver Long John
    Dunn was a tall lanky Texan with a tobacco-stained
    mustache and a slow droll nasal drawl.
He built his bridge in the Rio Grande Gorge just above the
    confluence with the Hondo river, basaltic cliffs
    channeling both rivers, wild rugged canyons.
Cliff swallows built their mud nests under the protective
    projections of the basalt, white-throated swifts whizzed
    up and down stream, herons waded in the water,
    mergansers dove for fish.
Like the swallows Long John Dunn built a stagehouse under
    a roof-like ledge, shelter in case of storm or accident,
    coffee, bacon and eggs, broiled steaks, bread, pie.
The bridge had a log caisson in the middle of the river,
    heavy basalt blocks piled into it, rock piers buttressed
    against the dirt banks below the cliffs,
And he scooped a zigzag road up the talus on the west cliff,
    connecting with the narrowgauge railroad at Servilleta.
His bridge survived the tumultuous torrents of spring and
    cloudbursts of summer. He relinquished it to a younger
    man, took work in town.
He married the maverick daughter of a rich rancher, turned
    her loose to pasture, married a neat native woman of
    Spanish descent who bore him three tomboy daughters
    and one studious son.
His children educated him. He was a fond father, gentle with
    horses, dogs, and kids, somewhat suspicious of women.
    His wife treated him tactfully, wore white gloves.
He secured an offical job mail carrier between Taos and the

railroad at Taos Junction, a precipitous road over a new
bridge across the Rio Grande.

He carried passengers as well as mail in his old Studebaker,
scaring them speechless as they descended or ascended
the tilted-shelf road along the sides of the cliffs, icy in
winter, dangerous at any time.

When a big storm washed out the approaches to the bridge
for a whole week, the mail undeliverable, irate house-
wives, not speechless, assailed him at the Taos post
office.

"Oh Mr. Dunn," one put the whole blame for the week on
him, "this mail situation is becoming intolerable!" He
looked down at her from his six-foot altitude and
drawled, "Ain't half so bad as the female situation,
ma'am."

He carried emergency cases all the way to the hospital in
Santa Fe in his old Studebaker, carried food to desperate
families, built his house in Taos as strong as he had
built his bridge, one of the best in town.

Tall tales were told about Long John Dunn after he died,
the memory of his lean lanky figure and slow droll
drawl lingering like a signpost of the past.

RADIUM SPRINGS

Very hot water, it seemed to issue out of molten lava at the
  edge of the river, a steaming pool, the fabulous Radium
  Springs.
Whether radioactive is controversial, reputedly it is a cure
  for rheumatism, tuberculosis, trachoma, venereal
  diseases, cancer, and general hypochondria.
An Englishman named Arthur Manby, supposedly a
  remittance guy having Warwick Castle connections,
  acquired it, built a stone hut around it, and his name
  was attached to it, Manby Springs.
Mabel Luhan and the sex-god D.H. Lawrence bathed there,
  but after Manby's head was severed from his body,
  though supposedly it was someone else's head and body,
  the name reverted to Radium Springs.
Then a farmer found the survey stakes were wrong, the
  springs really belonged to the Martinez heirs, so he
  payed the heirs and got title to the Springs, raised
  mushrooms in the steam heat.
A blight demolished the mushrooms, the farmer went back
  to farming, and another mysterious Englishman,
  supposedly the illegitimate son of King Edward,
  acquired the Radium Springs.
Naked promiscuous Hippies washed off their effluvia in the
  thermal pool, a sex-god would have been superfluous,
  the oldtime Taosians shunned them.
The Taos area seethes with hot springs, one at the mouth
  of the Arroya Miranda of moderate temperature, the
  hottest one up canyon from Pilar toward Picuris,
  commercial bathing at Ojo Caliente.
The largest volcanic crater in the world, eighteen miles in

61

diameter, is now the dormant Valle Grande, but the
Jemez Hot Springs bubble out of its lower walls.
Volcanos, earthquakes, nuclear explosions, no telling what
will happen any minute, population explosions already
exhausting natural resources, the lemmings of Norway,
Malthus.
The sun itself is a perpetual nuclear explosion reciprocally
regaining the energy lost, a self-winding apparatus, no
entropy to it, we may be radioactive ourselves wielding
atomic lasers and Occam razors trying to adjust. Hoo
hoo, birdie!

MANITOU

Manitou the Great Spirit pervading the forces of nature
Huaca, Orenda, Wakan similar Indian nomenclature
A power to utilize for food, strength, well-being
Invisible power to go with agreeing
Always there
Available without ritual or prayer.

PRAYING MANTIS

What does the praying mantis pray for?
Why, for prey to prey on, of course.
What do we people pray for?
Give us this day our daily bread,
Food for the stomach, wine for the head,
Kill sheep and cattle for plenty of meat,
Health, wealth, and happiness, eat eat and eat,
Kill other people who get in our way,
Pray for survival, pray pray and pray.

THE IRRECONCILABLE INTERNECINE

Cat mauling a mouse, goshawk clutching a quail, piranhas
   ripping the flesh off a man reducing him to a skeleton
   in a jiffy,
Man slaughtering animals, man slaughtering man, tribe
   against tribe, nation against nation, religion against
   religion, ideology against ideology.
Holy Roman potentates put out the eyes of nightingales so
   they would sing blind, castrated choir boys so they
   would sing treble,
Coyotes kill cats *and* mice, sportsmen kill coyotes for their
   pelts and for a bounty.
Kill kill kill, breed breed breed, perpetuate the strife of
   life, the irreconcilable internecine.
Jainists trample living things underfoot, vegetarians yank
   living plants out of the ground, crush cook eat.
'Tis a pitiless cosmos, existence consumed by existence, eon
   consumed by eon, to what end, purpose, power, glory?
We cannot transcend, we can only confront, resolve, create.
Compassion is always there with the paradoxical pair
Good and evil, right and wrong, truth and beauty.

LIE DETECTOR

The Berkeley poet Charles Keeler named his son Lëonarde
   after Leonardo da Vinci, hoping he would emulate the
   great man's versatile genius.
Keeler himself had considerable genius, renowned as an
   ornithologist as well as a poet, and he publicized
   himself considerably.
He had written a book on bird coloration in his twenties,
   his *Sequoia Sonnets* was a best seller, and he was a civic
   leader.
A sincere idealist nevertheless, his objective to make Berkeley
   the Athens of America, instrumental in building a Greek
   theater on the University of California campus.
He built his own home in a live-oak glade by an alder
   creek, planted pines and redwoods, made an outdoor
   theater, put on plays, poetry readings, concerts.
His wife was a resonator for his enthusiasms, corrected his
   excesses, an inspiring mother for his children, inspiring
   influence to her neighbors, everybody who knew her
   loved her.
She played the piano very well, a sensitive interpretive
   touch. She had young Lëonarde take flute lessons,
   accompanied him, instructed him on nuances.
Her elder daughter Merodeen was an artist, Eloise the baby
   of the family a writer, dancer, reciter, both sisters
   good companions for Lëonarde, and he grew up in a
   talented atmosphere.
His father taught him the common and Latin names of all
   the Berkeley birds, took him on excursions to the ocean
   beaches and coves for a study of sea birds.
He was an instinctive naturalist, picked up lizards, skinks,

71

king snakes, gopher snakes, kept a pet wildcat cageless
in the house.

He caught a broken-legged kitten in Redwood Canyon, taped
and mended the leg, a pettable pet, rather rough on
dishes when it jumped on the table.

"What's Nard Keeler up to now?" his neighbors pondered,
his eager earnest face, inquisitive affectionate eyes,
ingratiating grin exculpating him welcome in any
Berkeley household.

He won the hearts of high school girls with his flute playing.
They went for him, shied him away from adolescent
ardor.

In his senior year at high school he organized the John Muir
Club with three other boys, a staunch foursome, rivals
of the Sierra Club, sponsored by his father and Dr.
William Badé, president of the Pacific School of
Religion, John Muir's biographer.

They chose physicists, geologists, botanists as supervisors and
instructors for their hiking trips in the mountains,
charged high rates for the six or seven boys they took
with them.

Graduating from high school he majored in anthropology at
the University of California, fascinated by the intellect
of his father's friend Alfred Kroeber.

The sudden death of his mother changed his interest, a
terrific shock. He thought of carrying on her spirit with
music, a composer, his improvisations on the flute
already testifying his da Vinci versatility, but when his
father married again he felt like a lost child.

His sisters felt the jolt too. It was a marriage of convenience
and their stepmother did her best to cajole them but
Merodeen set up a studio of her own and Eloise, though

73

she stayed with her father, set up a world of her own, wrote poetry, joined a Little Theater group.

Lëonarde transferred to Stanford, majored in psychology, practically a pre-med course, rented a convenient redwood shack at the rear of a botany professor's house.

He cooked for himself or ate at restaurants, drove a second hand Buick sedan, the tonneau big enough to load his paraphernalia.

He missed his mother acutely. She had been the pivot of his projects in Berkeley, he could talk things around with her.

She had provided for him in her will, leaving him a goodly portion of her own inheritance, he spent freely.

The professor had been bitten by a rattlesnake while researching the hills behind Stanford, suction, incision, bleeding the usual remedy.

Which gave Lëonarde the idea to raise rattlesnakes for an anti-venom project. The professor concurred and they built a snake cage next to the redwood shack.

Lëonarde caught bagsful of rattlers in the coast hills, crotalus oreganus, imported red diamondback snakes, crotalus rubra, from the San Diego hills.

One of his John Muir Club friends had settled in Julian. Zoological, he teasingly enjoyed crating big ones, very aggressive.

Lëonarde would walk in the cage, let a rattler strike at the sole of his shoe, quickly pin its head down with a forked stick, pick it up by the neck.

Then he would let it bite through a membrane over a glass jar "milk" the venom from its fangs into the jar, have the venom injected in a horse.

By degrees, immunizing the horse and providing the blood

serum for the anti-venom. He made money, shared it with the professor.

His reputation at the university was as striking as his snakes, and he assimilated textbook knowledge at a glance, his da Vinci genius apparent.

Two co-eds at the university were very much attracted to him, he to them, and he contemplated marriage.

His father advocated early marriage to offset physiological and psychological frustrations. Both girls filled the bill on both scores.

Arlene Mac Leish had a beautiful body and encyclopediac mind apprehensive of psychological problems.

She had clean, clear, honest brown eyes, wispy brown hair, wore simple one-piece dresses with a small belt, never exposed but they couldn't conceal her very nice figure.

She came from a wealthy San Mateo family, her brother a polo player. She rented an upstairs room in a Palo Alto apartment house, a social lobby.

Rebelling against her family wealth she wanted to make something of herself, didn't drive a car, walked to the university.

Like Lëonarde she ate at restaurants, often together, he liked to talk wit her, a pragmatic idealist well-grounded in philosophy, psychology, history, literature.

She had read his father's poetry, critical of the triter poems, liking the later ones, and had heard about his famous book on bird coloration.

Lëonarde promised to show her a copy someday, the entire edition nearly destroyed in the earthquake and fire of 1906. His father refused to have it reprinted.

Deborah Dexter was an artist, a compact little body, piquant pretty face, violet eyes, dark hair bushed back in a

vertical furl, smooth serene forehead.

He took her on a bird-walk around the huge Stanford campus, imitated some of the songs for her, got her excited, told her about his father's book on coloration.

She invited him to Sunday dinners with her family, a comfortable family, her father an architect-contractor, her mother prettier than she was, capable, wholesome.

She was an only child, precious to them. They gave her an Essex coach to negotiate her classes. Her art teacher Pedro de Lemos advised them she had real talent.

Lëonarde was smitten with her painting of a majestic valley oak tree hanging in the parlor. As good as Merodeen's work, less definite, more impressionistic.

Arlene condescended to ride in his car with him to see his rattlesnakes, interested in the project. Deborah detested snakes, a bird girl.

It was an odd triangle. He couldn't decide which girl he wanted to marry, conceitedly believing both wanted to marry him.

His best friend Ralph Tant, one of the cofounders of the John Muir Club, came for a visit affording him the chance to test *his* reactions.

Introducing him first to Arlene in the lobby of her apartment house he got a surprising reaction. Ralph fell for her.

"Arlene, this is my friend the Right Reverend Ralph Burropacker. Ralph, this is Miss Arlene Mac Leish, the quintessence of feminine pulchritude."

"We have to tolerate his wisecracks, Ralph," she responded. "It's a congenital disease. But you know very well, Nard Keeler, that my name is pronounced Mc Clish, not Mack Leish."

"Ma Clish Ma Clush," Nard chanted, "Ma Thish Ma Thush,

79

Ma Hish Ma Hush, Ma Tish Ma Tush, Ma Gish Ma Gush, Ma . . ."

Ralph looped an arm around his windpipe. "Shall I throttle him for you, Arlene?"

"No, let him live. He's harmless. He can't help making rhymes, His father is a poet, you know."

Ralph was a violinist. Arlene twanged all the strings of his soul. He went for her avidly, found her intellect too formidable, desisted departed.

Lëonarde was left with the same triangle problem, cautious because of Ralph's reaction.

Before graduating the next year an event occured that settled the matter once and for all, a turning point in his life.

He brought the copy of his father's book on bird coloration to prove his father was more than a mere poet, a rare copy, his mother's name in it, an heirloom.

Arlene grasped the psychological impact of light effects, Deborah was impressed with the idea of protective coloration.

Meticulous with his projects, careless of his personal appearance and personal belongings, Lëonarde left the book on the front seat of his car at his usual parking place.

Returning he discovered it was gone, obviously stolen by someone interested in ornithology.

Arlene was very concerned. There were no thieves on the Stanford campus, only a psychopath could have taken it. Look for behavior clues.

Deborah was sympathetic. It was his mother's copy, her handwriting in it. No reason for anyone to take it. A kleptomaniac maybe.

A week later he saw the book on the front seat of Deborah's

Essex parked in the usual place near his.

He waited by her car, pulled the book off the seat, held it up accusingly in his left hand. Why did you take it, Deborah?

She gasped astounded, indignant, furious, tried to snatch the book away from him. He grabbed her with one arm, pulled her against him, their bodies agglutinated, a mystic sensation.

He flung her aside, went to tell Arlene. She was not surprised. She had suspected Deborah from the start. He waited by Deborah's car the next morning, told her what Arlene said.

The violet eyes flamed with hatred. "She took it herself and planted it in my car to make you think I took it.

Please believe me, Nard! I didn't do it! I love you! Damn Arlene, I'll tear her to pieces!"

She got in her car to quiet her hysteria, locked the doors against him. To hell with her, to hell with Arlene, to hell with all women!

He cleaned up his snake cage, quit college, got his diploma by mail, returned to Berkeley.

His father and stepmother were rather amused by his account of his quandary over the two girls.

"What you need is a lie detector, my son. They have one now at the police station. Dr. Larsen invented it. I think it would intrigue you."

It did. Dr. Larsen, M.D., was Lieutenant Larsen with the Berkeley police department, his father's friend.

He showed Lëonarde how the machine worked, predicted it would revolutionize the judicial system, eliminate costly court trials and costlier attorneys.

He said it was simply a super-sensitive pulse recorder, you

could try to fool your mind but you couldn't fool your heart.

From a blood-pressure armband a tube extended to a diaphram mounted on a revolving roll of graph paper.

From the metal-ringed diaphram a hooked pencil extended onto the paper and registered the pulse beats.

Normally the pulse beats made a wavering zigzag pattern to any question asked.

But when a lie was told the pencil jerked in a sidewise V to the margin of the graph paper.

The questions had to be direct requiring a straight yes or no answer. It seemed infallible. It fascinated Lëonarde. Dr. Larsen recruited him.

They made improvements, Lëonarde suggesting a hollow hooked glass needle filled with ink instead of a hooked pencil.

It transmitted vibrations from the diaphram onto the graph paper with less friction, like "milking" the venom from the fangs of a rattlesnake through a membrane into a glass jar, he tangently analogized.

Dr. Larsen was more interested in medical diagnoses of criminal behavior than mechanical deduction. He helped Lëonarde develop and patent a machine of his own.

And Lëonarde became known as the inventor of the lie detector despite his vehement denials giving Dr. Larsen full credit.

He organized a private detective agency expanding from Berkeley to Chicago and New York, his central head-quarters in Chicago.

Very profitable. Business men, Government officials, husbands, wives, gangsters consulted him with discreet trial cases.

Al Capone brought a lady he suspected of two-timing him.
  Lëonarde proved her innocent and Capone befriended
  him.
Lëonarde's secretary was a handwriting expert useful in
  clinching forgery cases. She was also an aviatrix as
  venturesome as he was.
Not so attractive as Arlene Mac Leish or Deborah Dexter
  she was nevertheless nice-looking and dependable and
  propinquity led to marriage, no children.
During the war they were kept busy on sabotage and spy
  investigations, and after the war the communist threat
  was more insidious than the Hitler threat.
Whittaker Chambers voluntarily came to him and requested
  a lie detector test on the yes or no rightness of his
  accusations against Alger Hiss.
He ran a clear record. Lëonarde informed Richard Nixon and
  the notorious trial for perjury began.
He was involved behind the scenes in a succession of
  publicized trials, the Lindberg baby case, the Oakes case,
  his testimony freeing Oakes.
But the lie detector was never admitted a legal instrument
  though police departments made use of its recordings.
He collaborated with the mystery story writer Erle Stanley
  Gardner establishing a Court of Last Resort. His ideal
  was to free the innocent rather than convict the guilty.
A world-famous criminologist, the sordidness of the
  situations he dealt with palled on him, he introspected
  why he was doing what he did.
It palled on his indispensible secretary and wife Catherine
  too. She wrote most of his letters for him, supervised
  the tests on morbid women clients.
She became morbid herself,and she was depressed by an

impending hysterectomy, afraid it would de-womanize her.

Lëonarde couldn't determine whether it was an accident or deliberate suicide when she crashed her airplane full speed against an Allegheny mountainside.

He felt he had neglected her in his preoccupation with other people and his own career.

He put a mental lie detector test on himself, did he love his egregious self more than he loved her, and was it love and what was love?

Nostalgia for California struck him hard, his family home in Berkeley, the live oak glade by the alder creek, his genteel intuitive hospitable mother, his poetic father, companionable sisters.

White crowned sparrows singing in spring, golden crowned sparrows singing in autumn, his favorite bird, and the olive-sided flycatcher calling from the tip of the redwood tree.

The Stanford chapel was another pivot, a beautiful chapel inside and out, the mosaic facade, a place to worship in without being religious.

And Deborah Dexter's virginal violet eyes drawing him into their purity, that one fierce mystic moment her body united with his.

She was more than a phantom of the past. What had become of her? He wrote his oldtime John Muir Club friend asking him to look her up.

Ralph replied she had married an artist she didn't know was homosexual, divorced him, moved to Carmel, painted seascapes, landscapes, portraits of children.

Go get her! Reclaim her! Start your lives over! Fate intervened. He was found dead in his car on a lonely

road north of Chicago.

He had been working on a conspiracy case. The F.B.I.
investigated, declared his death due to natural causes,
coronary thrombosis.

His agency partner declared it murder, a whiff of cyanide
leaves no trace, and continued with the conspiracy case.

Continued with the agency, testing thousands of willing or
manipulative clients on the Keeler polygraph.

LAZULI BUNTING

A loveable little bird the Lazuli Bunting
Nesting in the wild rose and wild plum thickets
His bright song and soft colors brown white blue
Blend melodiously and lazulate you.
A loveable little bird, lovelier than a linnet
His warble with a sweeter intonation in it.
He intimates the sky
Is far too high to fly
Stay in the thickets thou knowest
Brighten wherever thou goest.

EMPATHY

A beetle on its back waving its legs in the air,
Trying to turn over
The frightened eyes of a dog in a thunderstorm,
Shivering, whimpering
A child's eyes shining with eagerness and joy
A child's cry hurt beyond healing
Empathy with the aspirations and sufferings of all living
    things
Ride the wild mustang in the desert distance
Singing to the beat of its unshod hoofs.

AMULET

Amulet carved in turquoise
Ideas, ideals to live for
Creed code vow
Carved in the heart and mind
Stronger than stone
To share or hold alone.

ABOUT THE AUTHOR

Phillips Kloss was born in Webster Groves, Missouri in 1902.
His first acquaintance with New Mexico came in 1916 when
he worked on his brother's ranch. In 1925 he graduated from
the University of California at Berkeley. Two years later
he was back in New Mexico, this time with his wife,
Alice Geneva Glasier (Gene Kloss). In the years that followed,
living both in New Mexico and on the coast of California,
Mr. Kloss established himself nationally as an important poet
and critic. Phillips and Gene Kloss now live and work in
Taos, New Mexico. In addition to this volume, Sunstone
Press has published *Selected Poems, The Great Kiva, Gene Kloss
Etchings* and *Rainbow Obsidian*. Reviewers have called Kloss "an
idealist, and a poet with a distinctive voice."

www.ingramcontent.com/pod-product-compliance
Lightning Source LLC
Chambersburg PA
CBHW031144090426
42738CB00008B/1216